THE ENTREPRENEUR'S PLAYBOOK

HOW ENTREPRENEURS LIKE YOU ARE BUILDING DIGITAL BUSINESSES RIGHT NOW

RAY BREHM

DAUNTLESS

THE
ENTREPRENEUR'S
PLAYBOOK

RAY BREHM
and 14 successful entrepreneurs

CONTRIBUTORS

Ray Brehm, Jesse Kuhn, Paul T. Neustrom, Charylle Wolfe, Victoria Collette Jones, Flo Trouché-Curreri, D Lee Cutler, B Harrison James, Rachel J. Becquer, Kris Garlewicz, Violet Meuter, Matt Cooper, Dane A. Deutsch, George Lui and Paul G. Brodie.

CONTENTS

TIN CUP SYNDROME

BY RAY BREHM

I n the 1996 film, *Tin Cup*, Kevin Costner plays *Roy "Tin Cup" McAvoy*. He is a *"washed-up golf pro, working at a driving range"* who decides to try out for the US Open.

His rival (starting back in his college days) is Don Johnson's *David Simms,* who is a successful tour player. He is set up as the villain of the film. He is successful, arrogant and on the pro tour. He has the girlfriend (Rene Russo's *Dr. Molly Griswold*) who McAvoy is interested in as well.

Spoiler Alert

The famous closing scene reveals Tin Cup trying to hit over the water on the 18th hole from around 200 yards, while still in contention to win. He does this in lieu of laying up before the water. Instead of doing what a normal golfer would, he just *"goes for it."* He proceeds to hit each subsequent shot in the water.

On his 12th swing, he is down to the last ball in his bag, which means he is disqualified if that goes in the water. He hits it into the hole from that 200 yards out and ends up with a 12 on the hole. It is amazing, but he blew his chance to win the famed US Open.

End Spoiler.

That last scene is enjoyable to watch, to which Griswold claims McAvoy's 12 is *immortal.* It is also completely unrealistic.

In fact, my favorite line of the movie comes from the so-called villain.

Earlier on the course, Roy makes a double bogey on a hole. Simms rubs him a little.

> SIMMS: *Nice double, Roy.*
> TIN CUP: *Just keep making pars, a@$$&#!!*
> SIMMS: *I'll take eighteen of 'em.*

Even though we root for "Tin Cup" (McAvoy) in the movie, we should listen to David Simms.

He knows that success comes from small wins and

consistency. Aka hitting pars (and birdies). Not swinging for the fences.

I hear that quote in my head when I feel impatient, or feel like taking an unnecessary risk.

I'll take 18 pars, all day long.

I am not saying not to take risks, that is part of the game as an entrepreneur. But one should not take the Tin Cup style risks, that are unnecessary or serve no real purpose other than an ego boost.

This also goes for self-reflection. Many times we look at our results and say:

* *I didn't get enough leads (or email addresses)*
* *I didn't make enough sales*
* *Not enough people showed up to my webinar*

And I can tell you, I was that way for a long time. Then I realized that most of the successful people I looked up to, focused only on what they could control.

And that was...

Making a little bit of progress each day. Just keep moving forward.

In other words, to use sports terms:

* *hitting singles* in baseball (not swinging for the fence every time up) or
* *making pars* in golf (not trying to 'Tin Cup' it over the water).

Nowadays, I only worry about what I can control.

If I host a webinar, some weeks I will have 100s on live. Some weeks I may have 10. I don't worry about the number, I can only control my delivery of the material.

I don't worry about the number of emails I add to my list after any particular summit. That number will always fluctuate.

I can control creating and scheduling the next summit. If I keep hosting them, my list will continue to grow. It does not matter if any individual event grows by more or less than the prior event.

I'll take 18 pars all day long.

I really enjoyed *Tin Cup*, and sometimes the best advice comes from the villain.

Ray Brehm is USA Today and Wall Street Journal Bestselling Author, and the founder of Pubfunnels™, the #1 Business Hub For Authors. You can connect with Ray at raybrehm.com *or learn about Pubfunnels at* pubfunnels.com.

2

AUTHORITY LAUNCH: TRANSFORM YOUR STORY WITH THE PUBLISH-SPEAK-PROSPER PLAYBOOK

BY PAUL T. NEUSTROM

At its heart, entrepreneurship is a complex journey woven together by the struggle of vision and resilience, creating a powerful story. Over time, I've come to appreciate many successful entrepreneurs' strategies, like Alex Hormozi's best-selling book *$100M Offers*. It is an excellent example for others looking for a playbook to reach greatness.

Unlocking success requires more than simple business strategies; it requires tapping into your individual story to ignite inspiration and foster meaningful connections with others. Through my journey from homelessness to founding the Publish, Speak, and Prosper Movement, I've witnessed firsthand how the power of authentic storytelling can elevate not only personal success but also create lasting change on a global scale.

Wow, I couldn't believe my eyes when I saw my two latest books ranked first and third on Amazon! Alex Hormozi's book was ranked second. It was a total shock, and needless to say, I was blown away. It was so unexpected that I stayed up until 4:30 in the morning wondering what had just happened.

This awe-inspiring experience, which left an indelible mark on me, occurred when I had the privilege of witnessing half a dozen of my books become number one bestsellers on Amazon.

Directly competing against Alex Hormozi was both challenging and humbling, but it turned out to be one of the greatest learning experiences of my life. It reinforced a powerful truth: When you embrace and share your authentic story, you don't need to feel overshadowed by anyone. Your voice and experiences can stand alongside even the most successful figures and still make a meaningful impact.

This chapter will guide you through the process of unlocking the power of your personal narrative, showing you how to turn your struggles into success by leveraging the principles of publishing and speaking. Through this journey, you'll learn how to stand tall, own your story, and create a lasting legacy—just as I did in my own journey from struggle to success.

Part I: Learning From the Titans – The Alex Hormozi Playbook

Success leaves clues, only a few entrepreneurial journeys are as instructive and inspiring as that of Alex Hormozi. From humble beginnings to amassing a net worth exceeding $100 million in less than a decade, Hormozi's trajectory offers a road map for aspiring and established entrepreneurs alike.

Despite financial struggles, Alex scaled fitness gyms and grew three companies to over $120 million, emphasizing adaptability in business. His success highlights the importance of adaptability and responsiveness in the business world.

Building and Sharing Wealth

In 2021, Alex struck gold! He made a fortune selling parts of his businesses and co-founding Acquisition.com, which is now worth more than $150 million. But it's not just about the money for Hormozi; he's passionate about giving back and helping other entrepreneurs succeed. Alex believes that true success means lifting others up with you.

His story shows us that adaptability is key to making it big. If you're an entrepreneur looking to follow in his footsteps, here's what you need to know: Be ready to switch gears when needed, brush up on your skills, and don't be afraid to make money from new possibilities.

Key Lessons From Alex Hormozi's Playbook

1. **Act on Passion:** Refined his approach while pursuing his deep-seated passion.
2. **Be Willing to Adapt:** Aligned his business models with evolving market needs.
3. **Leverage Expertise:** Transformed personal experiences into scalable solutions, boosting impact and income.
4. **Invest in Others:** Emphasized community building and shared success by supporting fellow entrepreneurs.

Tailoring your approach to align with innovators like Hormozi extends beyond mere imitation; it's about adopting their strategies and mindsets to achieve remarkable success. Entrepreneurs must learn to pivot, grow, become inspired, and refine their business models if they want to stay relevant and prosperous in today's marketplace.

Emulating these principles of pivoting will lay a solid foundation for entrepreneurial success.

Part II: From the Streets to the Stage: How I Found My Voice and Became a Thought Leader

Discovering your voice can often be the hardest step toward freedom.

Recently, after leaving a men's monastery where I had lived for two years, I became homeless, living in an abandoned church while striving to imagine an optimistic future for myself at over sixty years old. At such crossroads in my life journey, I struggled with feelings of self-doubt, uncertainty, and the fear that I had lost my way completely.

Have you ever found yourself feeling helpless, uncertain of your next steps, and overwhelmed by life? I can relate. I know firsthand how difficult life can be at times. I have felt it all too keenly myself. Hey, I totally get that change can be tough, and it's easy to feel overwhelmed when you're faced with little hope to transform your life. But listen, you've got this!

With a little bit of grit, determination, and a whole lot of belief in yourself, you can create a future that's full of meaning and possibilities. The power is in the words you speak to yourself.

Discovering Purpose in the Midst of Adversity

In this most difficult time, I sought refuge and clarity in this quiet little church. By reading classic books such as Viktor Frankl's *Man's Search for Meaning* and digging deeper into Scriptures like the Bible, I embarked upon an introspective journey that revealed profound truths—among them, that discovering my purpose was central to overcoming any obstacle that came my way.

I harbored a lifelong dream of writing a book that would

transcend generations, encapsulating the lessons and experiences that had shaped my life. Battling self-doubt and fears of inadequacy, I confronted the pervasive "Imposter Syndrome" that threatened to silence my story.

Growing up in a small rural town, I felt a strong desire for a more fulfilling and connected life. I decided to write a book to share my knowledge and wisdom with the world, hoping to inspire others to achieve their dreams.

Out of the darkest recesses of fear, *Death of a Yellow Page Salesman* was conceived. Through the process of completing the book, I discovered my true purpose and found my authentic voice. The book became a #1 International Bestseller in four countries, and a Top Finalist in the Global Book Awards.

It took me seven years to write that book, and it was the toughest thing I had ever done in my life. It however became a most rewarding experience—not just because of the recognition, but because I had finally confronted my fears. I discovered the fulfillment from inspiring others to take action through my story.

The success of my memoir was not merely a personal triumph but a testament to the strength of authentic storytelling and the powerful impact of embracing one's true voice. It demonstrated that our most profound struggles could become the foundation for our greatest contributions.

The Power of the Spoken Word

As I progressed with my writing, I began by expanding into speaking and podcasting through my podcast *Skyrocket To Success*, engaging in dialogues with well-known entrepreneurs and everyday individuals alike. Spoken words can inspire and amplify written ones, fostering deeper connections and extending reach exponentially.

Our voice is the most powerful force of persuasion, turning words into an undeniable source of influence and impact.

Once I took to the stage to share my message, the real magic occurred. Winning awards as an author helped build my credibility, but speaking my truth to an audience released an even greater power: *connection*. I realized storytelling through words opens doors to new opportunities and broadens my message's impact.

Through these platforms, my following increased 15X, and my authority as a leader solidified. I saw firsthand how sharing personal stories and insights can inspire and empower others on their journeys of transformation.

Insights From My Journey

1. **Purpose Drives Resilience:** Aligning with your purpose empowers you to weather challenges.

2. **Authenticity Fosters Connections:** Sharing genuine experiences forges meaningful connections and creates purpose and belonging.
3. **The Power of the Voice:** Writing and speaking together amplify reach, engage audiences, and increase influence.

A light bulb moment led to the creation of the Publish, Speak, and Prosper Movement, a supportive space for overcoming fears, sharing stories, and personal growth.

Part III: The Movement: Transforming Lives Through Authentic Storytelling

This movement is grounded in the idea that every individual has a unique story to tell, and that stories create a ripple effect of inspiration and accomplishment. The community we've built is a collaborative space where members encourage, uplift, and push each other to achieve more than they ever thought possible.

Publishing and speaking are connected paths for spreading knowledge, inspiring change, and amplifying voices. This platform unites the power of speaking and writing, empowering aspiring authors and speakers to become successful entrepreneurs. Our resources guide them in refining skills, sharing narratives, and achieving entrepreneurial success.

The core of our approach is the **V.O.I.C.E. framework,**

which encapsulates the essential elements of impactful communication:

- **Vision:** Clarify message purpose and impact.
- **Originality:** Showcase your individuality.
- **Inspiration:** Draw from experiences and insights to motivate others.
- **Creativity:** Craft content that wows and lasts.
- **Embodiment:** Walk the talk and practice what you preach.

In a highly competitive marketplace, standing out through your voice—both written and spoken—is critical to long-term success. Your voice is your most persuasive instrument, allowing you to connect with your audiences on deep emotional levels.

I will never forget the time when I was searching for purpose and meaning in my life in that little church. Six weeks after I left, I met a woman who fell in love with my voice. Before, I believed the power was in the pen. Now, through my wife, Cherise, I understand the powerful impact of your voice and the persuasiveness it holds.

Conclusion: Three Key Takeaways for Your Next Step

Entrepreneurial success is a journey woven by vision, resilience, and learning. It also requires effective communication. We can achieve profound success by studying the strategies of entrepreneurs like Alex Hormozi.

Sharing authentic stories through publishing and speaking creates connections and a path to prosperity.

1 Conquering Fears for Thriving Success:

At the heart of every significant achievement lies the ability to triumph over fear. Whether it's fear of failure, inadequacy, or rejection, conquering these insecurities is the gateway to realizing your true potential. Like my journey, you too can transform your fears into the driving force of your path, turning obstacles into stepping stones toward thriving success.

2 Discover and Develop the Power of Your Voice:

Your story and personal experiences are powerful tools. Through consistent practice, self-discovery, and nurturing of your authentic voice, you have an amazing power to inspire and profoundly impact others. Blending written and spoken words amplifies this effect, connecting with a more diverse audience. Embrace your voice as your most valuable asset, inspiring others to embrace their authentic selves while contributing to creating a better world.

3 Embrace the Journey to Prosperity:

Success isn't just counted in dollars. It's measured in a life lived true to your purpose, with a heart that knows fulfillment. Through the written word and the spoken truth, and with the right people by your side, you'll build more than wealth—you'll build something lasting. Something that matters. You'll leave your mark on others in ways that can't be erased. Growing yourself while giving back to the world around you, that's where the real journey lies. That's where you find what endures.

Now is the time to make your mark! Embrace your voice, share your story, and join a movement that's transforming lives. Build your platform, elevate your influence, and watch your business thrive.

Join us in the Publish, Speak, and Prosper Movement—a community for personal and collective empowerment.

Paul T. Neustrom is an award-winning, international best-selling author, speaker, and transformational coach who equips individuals with proven strategies. Let's take the next step together and unlock the tools for success today. Start your journey here: PaulT-Neustrom.com.

3

OH LOOK, SQUIRREL!

BY CHARYLLE WOLFE

"The successful warrior is the average man, with laser-like focus."

— BRUCE LEE

Have you ever had one of those moments when a subtle shift in your beloved's expression hits you like a brick, and not in a good way? That's how I felt when I was sharing an idea with my husband, who also happens to be my business partner, about adding another service to our existing business.

If I hadn't looked up when I did, I would've missed it: that ever-so-subtle change on his handsome face that told me all I needed to know. What was wrong with him? It was a great idea! It could add thousands to our bottom line.

And, why did I have this sick feeling in the pit of my stomach?

I knew something was off. My husband's reaction was a clear sign, but I couldn't quite put my finger on it. Was he deliberately trying to squash a life-changing idea, one that could catapult our business and our legacy to the stratosphere? That certainly didn't fit with his modus operandi. Or was I being swept away by the excitement of a new idea, losing sight of our main goals? This moment of clarity brought me face-to-face with what is known as shiny object syndrome.

Shiny object syndrome (SOS) is a term used to describe the tendency to be easily distracted by new and exciting opportunities. It's like when you see something glittery or sparkly and can't help but chase after it, even if it takes you off your original path.

In the business world, SOS often manifests when companies constantly shift their focus to the latest trends, new technologies, or fresh opportunities, hoping they'll be the next big thing.

Large and small businesses alike have fallen prey to SOS. Take Yahoo, for example. Once a dominant force in the internet space, Yahoo arguably lost its way by constantly pursuing new and diverse ventures without a clear, cohesive strategy. This lack of focus led to missed opportunities and a decline in relevance compared to competitors like Google and Facebook.

Similarly, this may have also played a role in Evernote's

diminished influence. The company expanded into multiple directions, diluting its core offering and frustrating users with a cluttered interface and unclear strategy. Multiple changes in leadership and losing its laser focus on what made it so popular also seemed to have contributed to its challenges.

Shiny object syndrome in entrepreneurs can be explained through neuroscience, particularly by examining the brain's reward system and dopamine function. When entrepreneurs encounter new opportunities, their brains release dopamine, a neurotransmitter linked to pleasure and reward. This makes new ideas feel irresistible, driving the need for novelty over existing commitments. This dopamine-driven behavior, rooted in the brain's craving for new stimuli, can overshadow ongoing projects and cause frequent shifts in focus.

High dopamine levels can impair the prefrontal cortex, the area responsible for decision-making and impulse control, making it challenging to prioritize long-term goals over immediate rewards. This increased dopamine activity leads to greater distractibility, causing entrepreneurs to jump from one idea to another without completing any of them.

Several common triggers can spark SOS, such as the overintegration of new technologies, a cutting-edge tool promising to streamline operations, or a hot new market trend everyone is talking about—even when they don't align with your business needs. While staying updated with industry developments is important, falling into the trap of chasing every new idea can derail your business and your relationships.

Psychologically, SOS is often driven by the fear of missing out (FOMO). The excitement of newfangledness and the allure of potential quick wins can make you feel like you need to act fast or risk being left behind. This sense of urgency often leads to relentlessly chasing new ideas, without giving existing strategies enough time to become profitable. As a result, you may struggle to build the stable foundation your business needs to be sustainable.

Entrepreneurs, visionaries, and creatives are particularly prone to being caught in SOS. One reason for this is that this group is typically more comfortable than most when it comes to taking risks, being visible, and trying new things.

In an entrepreneurial adventure, or small business, SOS might look like this:

Business Model Pivots: You frequently change the direction of your business, trying to adapt to every new market trend or opportunity that arises. You can't stick to one business model long enough for it to prove its viability. Or, you may find yourself constantly rebranding or repositioning your business in an attempt to stay current or attract new audiences, causing confusion among customers and diluting your brand identity.

Accumulation: You frequently and unnecessarily purchase tools, apps, subscriptions, or services. You justify this spending by labeling it "research" or trying to fit a square peg in a round hole and forcing it to somehow work in your existing project. Maybe you've purchased a few domain names and built their corresponding incomplete websites only to forget about them until you get the renewal notice in your email or see the charge on your credit card. In the same vein, your library, digital and otherwise, is littered with half-watched webinars, unlistened-to podcasts, and books on shelves you have yet to crack open.

Constant Skill Acquisition: You're on a relentless quest to acquire new skills. You've purchased several online courses, promising yourself to start tomorrow, or next week, definitely next month at the latest.

Chronic Idea Generation Without Execution: You spend a significant amount of time brainstorming new ideas, products, and services but don't follow through.

Stress and Anxiety are Constant Companions: The perpetual cycle of new incoming ideas, projects, and tangents often leads to deteriorating mental health, as the growing list of unfinished tasks and unrealized goals becomes a mountain you're unable to climb.

Diversifying Into Unrelated Ventures: You invest in side projects that are unrelated to your core business. You've somehow convinced yourself they will offer fast and/or big returns. Instead, you end up diverting time and attention away from your main business, which generates your income, while draining resources and potentially leading to financial instability.

Developing a Reputation of Unreliability: From the outside looking in, you appear unfocused, unable to prioritize, and untrustworthy as a business partner, damaging your relationships, harming your ability to build lasting collaborations, and limiting future opportunities.

Okay, so now you may have recognized that you're prone to falling victim to SOS. What can you do about it? Let's start with some simple strategies you can implement to overcome and get back on track—before you veer too far off course or get that knowing "look" from your significant other.

Periodically clean out your email inbox. I know it sounds simple, but this small task can make a big difference. Start by unsubscribing from newsletters and promotions that you know fuel your SOS propensities. There are both free and paid tools available to help keep your inbox clutter-free. When you eliminate distractions from your inbox, you're less likely to be tempted by sparkling new offers or ideas that divert your focus. Consider funneling all email through a shared business email inbox. Having another set of eyes on what's coming in may help with this.

Know yourself. If you know you struggle with this, install some guardrails to keep you on the road. If you're not sure whether this applies to you, seek an accountability partner. If you're serious, ask someone you trust to give you the truth, not just what you want to hear.

Establish a clear mission statement for your business and filter temptation through that declaration. This serves as your North Star, helping you stay focused on your core objectives.

Reflect on what else is going on in your life. Is it possible there is a season or transition that you are getting ready to enter or are currently in that is perhaps difficult, unknown, or unwanted? Is the next shiny object possibly a way for you to avoid dealing with this?

Schedule "free time." I know a couple who takes the last three days every month, plus the weekend closest to those days, off in a row. They use this time to spend with the family, decompress from their business, and let their imaginations run wild to indulge in glittery objects and ideas. They are disciplined the rest of their working time, but allowing this space to explore has been helpful, as it allows freedom for creativity and keeps them focused on running their business the rest of the time. By keeping things in their proper containers, they've come to realize those things that catch their eye are usually a passing fancy, and they're able to easily dismiss it as SOS rearing its ugly head.

Filter your idea through the lens of your core audience. Does it line up with your values, goals, and vision? For instance, adding a planner may be a very good idea to a course module on small business principles, and provide extra value, but do you need to make it anything else? Do you really need menus, coloring pages, and other trackers sprinkled throughout the planner, or are you just making it easier for your clients, audience, or community to fall prey to their own shiny object tendencies?

Ask yourself whether the shiny object or rabbit trail you're considering will truly add value to your bottom line. This could mean increasing revenue, expanding your reach in your target market, or building goodwill among your peers. If the answer is no, you might want to set it aside for later, categorize it as a personal interest, or revisit it at a future date. The key is to stay focused on what will genuinely contribute to your business in a meaningful, tangible, and measurable way.

The next step would be to determine if it's something your market really wants or is asking you for. Create a minimally viable product (MVP) and put it out there. If there's some interest or feedback, you may want to go a little further. That doesn't mean you drop everything else and create a new offer, but sometimes just doing that and knowing whether it's something that would be well received or not can keep you focused on more important projects. Consider pulling in your accountability partner, or curating a small focus group of existing customers, as they may be able to give you a quick and definitive answer before you spend a ton of time or resources.

Where do you struggle? What comes to mind as you read this chapter? What strategies could you implement that are unique to your situation in order to keep the creep of SOS at bay in your own life?

I find one of the keys to overcoming SOS is balance. Embrace your creativity and willingness to take risks, but with a clear sense of direction. Be mindful of traps like frequent business pivots, accumulating unfinished projects, and constantly chasing the next big thing. By focusing on what truly drives your business forward, you'll build a foundation that is both innovative and sustainable.

As you cruise through your entrepreneurial adventure, it's easy to get swept up in new ideas and opportunities. Remember, success isn't just about seizing new opportunities but also about discerning which ones truly align with your long-term vision. By balancing ingenuity with focus, you can turn potential distractions into purposeful actions.

Just as my husband's expression gave me pause, it's necessary to listen to those moments of hesitation and ask yourself whether this new idea truly aligns with your long-term goals. By staying focused on what matters most, you can avoid the pitfalls of SOS and keep your business moving steadily toward success. I've enjoyed sharing this topic with you and wish you the very best as you learn to manage SOS and achieve your greatest triumphs!

Charylle is a seasoned author, coach, and marketer, passionate about helping entrepreneurs thrive. Connect with her for insights, tips, and more at charyllewolfe.com.

4

CURIOSITY KILLED THE C.A.T.

BY VICTORIA COLLETTE JONES

O f all the skills I have acquired as an entrepreneur, the habit of curiosity has led to my most significant breakthroughs. By utilizing curiosity, I can avoid careless attitudes and thinking, enabling me to make better decisions and pursue more worthwhile goals. These conclusions are realizations I came to while preparing to write the chapter for this book.

My story began earlier this summer. It was a bright sunny day, although the air hung heavy with the scent of diesel fumes at the railway station of a small town in England. I glanced up occasionally while reading a book, awaiting my train.

As I read, one of the attendants at the station, who was picking up trash, approached me. He had kind eyes and a friendly face but wore a concerned expression.

"What are you reading?" he asked. "I am always interested to know what people are reading."

I glanced around and noticed a group of teenagers on their phones and a small family talking to their child. I realized that seeing someone reading a book must be quite a rare occurrence these days.

I happily conversed with the attendant, showed him the title of the book I was reading, and shared what it was about. He opened up and said he had recently read *The 48 Laws of Power*. While reading this book, he was shocked to discover that some people will sign a guest book with a false name. He also expressed how relieved he was when his wife was equally appalled when he shared the story. Her reaction had reinforced his faith in her. He then went on to exclaim that discovering his parents didn't know everything was one of the biggest shocks of his life!

I was totally charmed by the conversation, and I advised him there *were* good people in the world; you just need to know how to identify the bad ones. He nodded at me as he took his leave, still looking slightly stunned, and said, "I appreciate you!"

This unprompted conversation left me reflecting on the beauty of trust in uncorrupted, almost childlike human beings. At the same time, I reflected on how unfortunate it is that these qualities have been sullied and taken advantage of over time.

Childlike innocence is a wondrous thing but a dangerous quality in adults.

I never wanted to be cynical. Indeed, my trusting nature and inclination to hold on to goodness and moral values have largely protected me. When my compass direction points toward true north, it is usually easier to sense any slight deviations in the magnetic field—although not always.

The problem, I find, arises when we are born into and educated into systems that we are told, with good intentions, have been set up for the benefit of everyone. Society tells us our safety and success rely on cooperating with such systems.

Finding out that is not the case can be quite a shock and is usually accompanied by a deep sense of betrayal that can be very difficult to recover from. Such a challenge can leave one feeling like everything they ever believed in, loved, and had faith in had all been a lie, and now everything would have to be rebuilt.

In the immediacy of the shock, it is easy to go to these extremes of feeling. Of course, cooler analysis demonstrates that not everything is a lie. Indeed, elements of the truth are needed. Otherwise, such systems would fall apart much sooner.

But truth mixed with lies is a much more treacherous combination. It is much more confusing to identify a lie and call it out when combined with elements of the truth. So, how do we determine the difference?

Why

Do you remember that annoying question your parents often shut down rather than answer as a child? I do. It is the question, "Why?"

Many of my "why" questions were left unanswered or dismissed as a child, but I never let that stop me. Whenever I could, I sought the answer to the question, "Why?"

Often, the answer would elude me for many years. The question was always lurking until a new piece of evidence encouraged me to pull the neglected half-finished jigsaw in my mind off its dusty shelf. I would then sit and analyze it with my newly discovered puzzle piece until I figured out exactly where it fit.

Of all the skills I learned as an entrepreneur, from the daily disciplinary tasks to the diet and exercise regimes, to the networking habits and carefully chosen advisors, it was my "why" questions that led to my entrepreneurial breakthroughs.

In my first book, *Truth Decay—How Bitcoin Fixes This*, I tell how my mother's fear of doctors led me to become a dentist, a profession I worked in for over twenty years. It was my curiosity as to "why" my mother suffered as she did that made me choose that profession over anything else. The constant "why" made me question how my predecessors set up my profession and why it proposed helping people in the way it did; my ultimate disillusion with those answers eventually made me leave.

Regarding curiosity and "why" questions, I apply my tactics in two main categories: systems and people.

Systems

When it comes to systems, it may sound obvious, but the first question I ask myself is:

What makes sense?

If the website of the United Nations tells me they are making increasing progress in solving poverty, but everyone around me seems to be progressively poorer— something doesn't make sense. So, I need to ask more questions.

I don't dismiss things I don't understand.

In a world of abundant knowledge, we are encouraged to delegate our trust and responsibility to specialists. Admittedly, it is hard to become an expert in everything, so recruiting specialists makes sense. But what if those specialists are wrong? What if they don't even know they are incorrect and want to bully me into believing they are right? To protect myself, I need some understanding of the subject I am asking them to help me with.

I don't make assumptions.

In a busy world, I have to take certain matters at face value, as I do not have time to analyze everything that confronts me. How many of us read the terms and conditions of the software updates regularly presented to us? I don't have time to do this, so the temptation is to assume that if everyone else agrees with them, then they must be okay. Otherwise, someone would surely have said something. What if someone *is* saying something, though, but I just haven't heard about it? Just thinking about the consequences in this scenario can become overwhelming.

I ask questions.

Realizing the danger of our assumptions is indeed draining. It is time-consuming to try and comprehend all of the possible consequences. However, I find the effort is worthwhile. As an individual entrepreneur, I am up against large organizations that run on specialization and carefully crafted assumptions. Understanding where some of the fallacies lie can give me the stone for the slingshot as I face my proverbial Goliath.

I learn more.

I don't even need to know everything. Comprehending where just one misunderstanding lies can lead me to the next one and then the next. In a world where those who question are still in the minority, it wasn't long before my understanding was head and shoulders above many others. The one disadvantage of all this advanced knowledge is that I start to feel a little lonely because fewer and fewer people around me can understand when I am discussing specific topics.

People

Sadly, we live in a world where only some people are genuine and trustworthy. Good business relationships, networks, and successful schemes rely significantly on trust. When evil people undermine trust, matters can go south quickly. So, how do we assess people and maneuver around the bad ones successfully? Many of us have come to rely on legal systems, but these days, even these systems can prove unreliable and unworthy of pursuing because of the cost of resources. Not just financial resources but also mental and emotional. Reducing the need for such sabotaging actions requires us to be able to assess people efficiently and accurately.

Look Beyond the Superficial

We live in a world designed to seduce us. Beauty, charm, and flattery are characteristics often attributed to good people. However, knowing this, those who want to achieve the advantages of being seen as good can create a superficial veneer to claim the benefits of such qualities.

Con artists often use sweet words and flattery to convince

us of something. So, in my world, an excellent first step is to be suspicious of anyone who is overcomplimentary and to consider how they might want to take advantage of me rather than just assuming that they are a nice person who wants to give me something.

Values

Assessing the values of others will always be a tricky but essential skill. I do not want to offend the innocent, but at the same time, I need to protect myself from those with nefarious intentions. In guiding my teenage daughter, I advise her to be more curious about people and judge them by their actions, not by what they say. If someone says they will do something, then they don't deliver—or, even worse, deny all knowledge of their promise—this gives you important information about a person's character. As a wise person once said, believe them when someone shows you who they are.

While forgiveness and compassion are essential, offering these gifts to the wrong people in business slows me down and compromises my success. In addition, I want to avoid confusing others and causing them to doubt my integrity by being clear in my actions. I consider that astute others who wish to partner with me in business also assess me for the qualities I look for in others.

C.A.T.

In the process of asking and looking for answers to some of these questions, and after ten years as a dentist working for others, I set up my own dental business. Running my own business led to asking and answering questions on a whole new level. In my book, I talk about how the financial crisis of 2008 challenged me in ways I never imagined, leading me to ask and answer even bigger "why" questions, which led me to the work I do now, writing and speaking about the history of finance, and Bitcoin as a new solution to the problems in our current monetary system.

Even with this, my curiosity still stands unabated. I have many unanswered questions, but as I discover more answers, I write about them, as I am doing here and on my website, SatoshisPage.com.

It is difficult for a train to reach its destination when it relies on broken train tracks or those tracks lead in the wrong direction, which is why I believe every entrepreneur needs the habit of curiosity. Because curiosity doesn't kill the pet cat; it kills the C.A.T.—that is, Careless Attitudes and Thinking.

Victoria Collette Jones is a writer, speaker, and the author of Truth Decay—How Bitcoin Fixes This. You can find out more about Victoria at her website, SatoshisPage.com.

5

THE JOURNEY TO AUTHORPRENEUR SUCCESS
BY FLO TROUCHÉ-CURRERI

"Success is nothing more than a few simple disciplines practiced every day."

— JIM ROHN, AUTHOR AND MOTIVATIONAL SPEAKER

Achieving success as an author entrepreneur involves mastering writing skills, becoming proficient in new abilities, consistent practice, adaptability to change, and willingness to take calculated risks. In today's digital age, the avenue to a prosperous career and business is more accessible than in the past.

Sometimes, we don't realize we are standing in our own way and blocking our chances of progressing in our author careers. I developed a more focused habit of learning and recognizing opportunities. Personal beliefs and lack of confidence or knowledge can prevent us from achieving our dreams.

When I started writing in the 1970s, becoming an author seemed like an elusive dream reserved for a select few. I believed that becoming an author meant writing a book and finding a publisher. Job done. After joining a writer's group, I found the focus to be on becoming published, not the business of becoming an author, such as copyrights, intellectual property, and taxes.

In 1992, I founded a quarterly parapsychological journal in order to become published and start my own business. Using a DOS-operated computer, I stepped into the roles of writer, editor, and publisher instead of hiring employees. Still, I didn't know how to turn the journal into a business. My distribution was by mail in the United States and internationally.

To gather subject matter, I attended conferences on the paranormal in Santa Barbara, Los Angeles, and Washington, D.C., and reported about the sessions. I exchanged my journal with other parapsychological publications and summarized their papers in layperson's language. I used a copy machine to print the issues and then switched to hiring a typographer. Although I tracked income and expenses for publishing and mailing, I didn't track travel, food, mileage, or ticket expenses to attend conferences. With fewer than twenty-five subscribers, I ceased publication.

Inventor Alexander Graham Bell once said, "When one

door closes, another opens, but we often look so long and so regretfully upon the closed door that we do not see the one which has opened for us." To reach my goal, I began to search for another door to open.

In 2022, I became overwhelmed after reading about publishing, beta readers, launch teams, and marketing. After enrolling in a publishing school to publish my book, I found that hiring editors, creating a launch team, obtaining reviews, and marketing my book remained my job. The program did not include information on how to start a business or make money as an author. I dropped out. The possibility of becoming published and having a successful business began to fade into obscurity.

But I set a goal to succeed, adopting a disciplined approach focused on skill development, embracing constructive criticism, seeking assistance when necessary, and evaluating opportunities to improve my skills.

Everything began to change when I received a transformative email.

The letter contained an offer to purchase a bundle of discounted courses and offers called a stack. The selections included courses and ebooks on marketing, email, attracting clients, business branding, and writing.

Joining the email lists of those who contributed to the stack resulted in emails with tips, personal stories, offers on products, and webinars. Email is a key ingredient in building a business. It was shocking to learn that my books were secondary to my business.

To become an author and an entrepreneur, I had to become what the industry calls an authorpreneur. Most authors don't make money by writing books—they sell products and build an email list to gain more clients.

The emails created a domino effect of opportunities. I learned that the primary part of the business is selling webinars, courses, and summit premium passes. Summits consist of various speakers being interviewed on a specific topic. Books have become business cards for the internet, given away or sold at a nominal price as an incentive to join a mailing list. After accepting one offer from the email, another would appear, each adding structure to the foundation of the previous one.

For example, the first course taught how to create a slideshow webinar with AI, and the second taught how to develop courses emphasizing market research. Asking people for feedback and to purchase the course unsettled me because I didn't want to be annoying or impolite. But being a businesswoman requires asking people to buy a product to acquire students and grow the email list and business.

"Commit yourself to lifelong learning. The most valuable asset you'll ever have is your mind and what you put into it," advised Brian Tracy, author and motivational speaker. Training never stops. Increasing knowledge and skill-building is crucial.

Before I finished the second course, another email arrived with an offer.

The third course demonstrated ways to set up video

presentations for a more businesslike appearance, building on the previous two courses. It recommended lighting, webcams, microphones, and backgrounds, increasing the professionalism of webinars and courses, with the prospect of attracting more students.

Taking calculated risks means evaluating offers by comparing the pros and cons and weighing the benefits, cost, and time required against need.

Sometimes, I stutter, have difficulty reading out loud, and need an AI voice that sounds close to human. I searched online for a realistic text-to-voice program. The program replaces my voice when I draft webinars and read manuscripts. The sound worked out well and was very close to sounding natural. This enabled me to consider creating numerous webinars and courses as the basis of my business. They could become evergreen courses, meaning the sales can be automated.

Learning how to write emails that entertain or contain tips and information can help you create more exciting content for your followers. Some of them may be requests for you to co-author a book, be a speaker in front of a group, be a podcast guest, or be a speaker at a summit. Each of these actions can help grow your email list, bring in new clients, and make your business grow faster. The more exposure you receive, the more people will recognize who you are and trust you.

Subscribing to mailing lists also provides opportunities not found elsewhere.

To avoid missing important correspondence, I use three services for different purposes. Outlook is reserved for family and friends, Yahoo is for anything I buy or subscribe to, and my domain address is reserved for business.

Reading emails that sound like the sender is a hot dog vendor producing a gamut of offers with little content or talking only about what they need instead of what they can do for you is a good way to learn how not to write an email. You want to grow a following, not lose them.

Emails often contain helpful information about new products, learning opportunities, and ideas for authors and their businesses. The offer most important to me is my membership in a hub service. A hub is a central connection for organizing a website, bulk mailings, podcasting, blogging, marketing, and platforms for creating courses and funnels to automate mail and sales in one place. I believe a hub is the key to creating a solid business.

In his great wisdom, Benjamin Franklin said, "The best investment is in the tools of one's trade." The author's hub, Pubfunnels, was my best investment because all my other services depend on it. Before knowing how to start my business, I invested in the hub, bought a domain name, and connected a website to it. With a book, webinar, course, and summit planned, I needed to add a shopping cart and a bulk mail service under my business name. These tools can help your business succeed, and mastering them is a priority.

Premium passes for summits provide access to videos for life, as do many courses, or a free limited-time video replay.

They are a good source for learning about marketing and other topics to help your business grow. Companies selling courses online, such as Udemy, also provide lifetime access to the course without additional fees. They consistently have a selection marked down from over a hundred to under thirty dollars.

Webinars can be prerecorded, live, or a mix of both. Check the description of what is offered and whether a replay is available. Reading the summary is advisable to avoid making a mistake. Sites like Udemy offer previews of lessons for evaluating the instructor's speaking pace, accent, and mannerisms. Try to avoid instructors with distracting habits.

Many years ago, I purchased a photography course on audiotape. The instructor would wave a handbell, producing an ear-deafening ringing sound. The noise became so irritating that I could not face going through another lesson.

YouTube is a great resource for learning. Many knowledgeable businesspeople and experts share tips on their channels on topics such as writing, marketing, and legal documents that outline requirements for websites and email. I follow a few channels myself. Their videos average between thirty and sixty minutes long.

"The ultimate victory in competition is derived from the inner satisfaction of knowing that you have done your best and have gotten the most out of what you had to give," said Howard Cosell, American sports journalist, broadcaster, and author.

Doing your best takes effort, and staying competitive requires keeping up with advancements. Learning new technology is worth the time and work it takes to make writing easier and faster, and make your business run more smoothly. Software, cameras, and sound equipment keep improving, and book cover designs change according to what is selling.

Sometimes, a lack of knowledge or time makes obtaining help necessary.

A do-it-for-you service is more expensive but can be used for tasks you don't like or are not proficient in performing. These companies produce better results than most authors do themselves. Their goal is to format, edit, and publish the book, create a cover, and market it to reach bestseller status.

Other tools include writing software for authors, such as AutoCrit, which includes tutorials, editing, and grammar-correcting processes. These tools can reduce the cost of hiring editors, saving businesses money. There are also programs to help authors self-publish, such as Atticus. In addition to being a writing tool, the program simplifies publishing by building many steps into the software to upload manuscripts to Amazon's Kindle Direct Publishing (KDP). Another publishing tool is Publisher Rocket.

Struggling through trial and error isn't necessary. Seek help when needed. Focus on practicing learned skills. Use tools like a hub's chat or onboarding calls for help with websites, shopping carts, bulk email, or setting up other services.

Staying open to unfamiliar ideas, being willing to put in a lot of effort and time, and, most of all, believing in yourself increases self-confidence. Joining local networking groups, speaking at summits or on stage, hosting podcasts, and interacting with other authors help build your business. It can also be a way to meet other entrepreneurs and receive tips and notifications on classes, courses, and seminars.

Success started to happen when I began developing alliances through email, engaging in enlightening webinars, and participating in impactful online summits and courses. The expansive internet offers a wealth of knowledge, much of it free, some for a nominal amount. These educational resources can be reached on any device with internet access. Verify content accuracy by comparing it with other sources on the subject.

It only took me one year to move from a place without direction to a structured place of co-authoring books, creating online courses, and hosting seminars.

Investing in my dreams by acquiring the tools to lay the foundation for my business, and seeking knowledge and opportunities, paved the way to my success. Anyone can follow a similar path with tools that help them to accomplish their goals and become successful authorpreneurs.

"If you can dream it, you can achieve it."

— ZIG ZIGLAR, AUTHOR AND
MOTIVATIONAL SPEAKER

Flo Trouché-Curreri is a bestseller author with experience in fiction and nonfiction writing and course creation. She is a member of The Alliance of Independent Authors (ALLI). You can contact Flo at https://trouche-curreri.com/freebie1

6

BALANCING DAILY MOMENTS
BY D LEE CUTLER

Every morning is an unfolding gift.
Connect your mind to your heart with a question as you ask,
"How do I feel today?"
In the space of a moment, take a long, deep breath.
Tune to melodic sounds of songbirds calling.
Stop whatever you are doing.
Simply listen.
Use all of your senses in this moment,
To open to the sight of the abundant light,
To be present to what shows up in front of your eyes,
To open your ears to hear the whispering breeze,
To open your nose to draw in the surrounding smells,
To feel the touch holding shared love,
To taste the gift of delightful flavors,
To feel the beat of my grateful heart.

Give each day a warm hug.
Share the blessings.
They are here. They are there.
Moments of joy are everywhere.
—dLee

W e each are given a certain number of moments. Each minute is made up of 60 seconds, there are 60 minutes in an hour, there are 24 hours in a day, and 24 times 365 days equals 8,760 hours in a year. Every day is a new opportunity to create balance and daily patterns with your precious time, and each day has a limited number of moments. We each have the same amount available to us to choose how to experience the moments. Moments can be easily wasted and set aside with an attitude of "I'll do it later." But how does the end of each day feel when you do this?

Structure and routines provide a habit that results in a flow of mental, physical, and emotional energy. I learned this growing up and observed this effect every day. My father chose to start and end each day with the routine of simply taking care of little seeds in his garden. Each seedling had a unique experience and possibility for survival, but those that lived shared a colorful flower, fruit, or more seeds as food for a variety of birds.

My father had a very stressful and demanding career. He took the time and divided the day into subsections, looking at the time slots like a balance sheet with important and valuable things he did both for himself and for his clients.

He started his day with moments spent in his garden or greenhouse taking care of the little seeds he was focused on at the time. While stressful, this daily habit resulted in 100 percent of the little precious seedlings finding a home. Observing this process, I was in daily awe of how it gave him a positive start to each morning when he came in from caring for the little seeds. He had a seed status story and a smile to share first thing in the morning before he headed out to his demanding schedule. I also observed that at the end of each day, my father took a few of his moments to water the seedlings and to closely inspect the changes that occurred during the day.

Each day is made up of many opportunities and choices. Ultimately, we need to be present in each moment within ourselves and clearly communicate how we want to combine the moments in order to make wise choices. We need to approach each moment and the resulting choices within *any* moment by starting to *feel,* first from our hearts rather than our heads. When you check in with your feelings, ask yourself questions: Is there joy? Is there love? Is there anxiety? Become aware of the sensations when you feel these emotions.

As you feel, you are being present in each moment and can make choices on what you want to focus on. It is similar to how a bee has to choose how many flowers to focus on to be successful collecting pollen and then return to the hive to share. The bee is in motion from flower to flower looking for nectar with a purpose.

Balancing the moments within each day and within each week helps to provide a daily and weekly habit of awakening with a commitment to being present. When you start your time with a specific purpose, it will feel good as you connect within yourself and make choices from your heart.

When you start each morning by getting your creativity going, it can add a special sweetness to your day. It helps to keep your energy up if you set up a small amount of items each day to work on for a certain amount of time, and then move on to the next. It is like the bee going to a certain number of flowers to collect the necessary nectar. You can follow this example and do something for a short period of time to keep it interesting and keep it moving.

How you spend your time, and how you trade it in for an experience, matters. I learned how to put an importance on having moments in my schedule to experience nature and feelings of awe.

Take your week and break the days into bite-sized time chunks to get important things completed. Ask yourself what you *want* to be doing rather than just reacting to what comes up. Starting each day from a higher perspective gives you a powerful sense of having a choice in how to focus and how to use your daily moments and limited time.

MONDAY: Be proactive and design your moments for the day and week to concentrate on your issues and concerns. You will be better prepared to help others.

TUESDAY: Work on a priority of tasks that need to be done. If they cannot be completed in this one day, spread them out for the rest of the week, breaking them down into something to be done each day.

WEDNESDAY: Work on projects that need to be shared and move them forward for review.

THURSDAY: Work on the ideas and necessary connections to the structure of any important areas.

FRIDAY: Feel what it is like to wrap up the focus of the week. Have a sense of release and joy in what you have accomplished.

SATURDAY: Slow down and reflect on the events of the week and what needs to be moved into the next focused time.

SUNDAY: Smell the coffee and the air. Pause and savor moments like these.

I learned the importance of observation and connection. The structure of balancing the daily moments with positive vibes resulted in a positive energy at the end of the day. It is important to use this habit consistently each day.

At the end of the day, do you feel like you can recall the emotions from your experiences? Is your first step to plan out the day and then move along during the day dealing with whatever unfolds however you can? When you start "being here now" and feeling from your heart, you will find the day's focus and flow will be easier.

Doing this requires a mindset shift to make it an experience rather than a task listed on your to-do list. When you start your day with a higher emotional perspective, it is possible to experience more moments of awe with joy and love. From this simple experience and powerful energy flow, it is possible to be aware of all the opportunities and potential. Because you have chosen to be present and connect with your feelings, the resulting focus and flow will greatly improve your day.

Savor This Moment: The Gift of Time
Give yourself the gift of time to pause, reflect, and refresh from the top of each day.
As you align yourself first as number one with your precious time,
Set your intentions to connect directly within yourself.
Your day will gracefully begin to flow smoothly until your evening hour ends.
As you practice presence in each moment,
Your intention will help get you where you want to go.
—dLee

dLee is an award winning nature photographer, founder of PhotodLights photo book collections on Amazon, creative entrepreneur and businesswoman with a positive attitude of "I can do this." You can connect with Donna at https:// dleephotodlights.com

7

THE SERVICE BUSINESS MENTOR
BY B HARRISON JAMES

How can any service business owner get more leads, keep customers longer, and sell more without spending any more on advertising than they already are? Read on to find out.

Common Questions Service Business Owners Ask

"Where can I go for help with my business?"

"How do I open a business bank account? Is anything negotiable?"

"What form of organization should I take? Sole Proprietor, LLC, Corporation?"

"How do I pay myself? My employees?"

"How can I get customers?"

I had all these questions (and more) when I started my accounting and tax preparation service business.

I didn't have any answers. I didn't know where to go for answers.

For compliance information, I visited the city licensing and tax authority, the zoning department, the state tax department, and the federal tax department. I had to dig through volumes of written materials to learn how to operate within the law, get customers, and keep business records.

I had always worked for an employer and received a paycheck (trading my time for dollars). I had never owned a business and didn't really have anyone to ask about what to do.

So, I bought a franchise, thinking that was the solution.

In their system, I was trained to help business owners with their records and taxes.

I was taught to find customers by walking into a business, offering them a "Tax Tips" booklet, and asking how they kept their books.

If they talked with me, we would proceed from there. This is an example of "interruption marketing."

It doesn't go over well now, and it's also a big waste of time—my time!

The Beginnings of a Solution

I finally learned (after much research, study, and experience) what worked better.

I discovered they'd talk with me if I offered something that answered a question or solved a problem.

Otherwise, they would say, "Not interested." And at that point, I had no relationship with those prospects.

Building Trust

But, if I had their first name and email address, I could send valuable information about how they could grow their business, attract more customers, and run their business more effectively.

That led to creating a business relationship.

If I only had known this from the beginning.

The lifeblood of a business is new customers because some die, some move away, and some go to other providers. Your business will fail if you don't have a constant flow of new prospects.

When I began, everything was done manually.

Now, several electronic tools are available to us to market more efficiently: email, webinars, podcasts, streaming services, etc.

One of the easiest ways to begin is by email.

This requires you to collect the names of your prospects and customers, develop a mailing list, and communicate with them regularly.

That way, you build authority, credibility, and relationships.

People do business with providers they know, like, and trust and who can provide solutions to their problems.

That should be you. You need a website.

Why a Website?

A website is a valuable tool. But I'm not suggesting just any website.

It should be a lead-capture website with an "About Us" tab. The tab should not tell the reader about you but explain what advantages and benefits they would get from working with you.

Your website should also include a "Contact Us" link with an email, phone number, and address. Your email address should be in the form of yourfirstname@yourwebsite.com. Not JohnSmith4478@gmail.com.

Many people want to check you out before they leave contact information. They can't check on you if your email address is from Gmail or Outlook.

Your Solution

ServiceBusinessMentor.com offers business help, answers to your questions, and business training.

Business training meetings are offered at least once monthly and usually last less than one hour.

Additional Q and A sessions are also offered monthly. Emailed questions are available at any time.

In addition to providing help with marketing, you also can get answers to business questions like those at the beginning of this chapter.

With over forty years in business, tax advisory and preparation, and education (I taught as an adjunct professor on the college level for three years), I am well-positioned to help you with your business operations and marketing.

If you want information on how I can help you, I give a free report called "How Any Service Business Owner Can Get Business Answers and Strategies at a Price They Can Afford." Go to ServiceBusinessMentor.com and request your free copy now.

I help service business owners attract more ideal prospects and boost sales using proven marketing and growth strategies to enjoy increased profits and lasting customer relationships. You can connect with me at ServiceBusinessMentor.com

8

IT TAKES A VILLAGE TO RAISE A STAR

BY RACHEL J. BECQUER

Welcome and aloha!
Mitakuye Oyasin. (We are all related.)
Pilamaye (I appreciate you) for being here.

Mission Statement

I am on a mission to green the earth, empower the autism community, rescue horses, and promote indigenous wisdom, by providing community, housing, and retreats in sustainable eco villages.

"Have a mission, take a stand."

— RYAN ELIASON, VISIONARY BUSINESS
MASTER

Vision

I envision paradise returning to the earth. I caught a glimpse of this when I was on the island of Kauai, attending my Visionary Business Mastery retreat in Hawaii. I was out on a field trip hugging trees with I., another visionary, when we met up with a native islander who was creating baskets, ingeniously and quickly, for the tourists.

As we talked, my heart opened to see the vision that I had seen as a child again: the earth, as it once was, green and lush and new again, serene and peaceful. We spoke of a new kind of people on the earth, a new way of being and seeing, which is really the old way, the original way, the blueprint we were designed with.

We visited a magical place the islanders had created for the tourists, as nature was back in the day before it was destroyed.

I can see it.

I envision eco villages being created all over the world as humanity transitions to this new earth. Each villager will own or lease their own tiny house and will share gorgeous community centers. The houses will be placed into octagon shapes, with a fire pit in the center of each of the octagons. These will be spread out over 600 acres, with bike paths in between these shapes. From the air, the honeycomb pattern and infinity patterns will be visible.

Therapies will be provided that have helped my own family, and others will come into being, as we will always be open to expand into new possibilities. Some of the main modalities will be RDIconnect (relationship development intervention and dynamic intelligence development program created by Dr. Steven Gutstein and Dr. Rachelle K. Sheely), EAGALA (which is equine therapy), HeartMath with horses, ESAs (emotional support animals), AIT (auditory integration therapy), sensory diet, forest bathing, nature therapy, art therapy, music therapy, martial arts, dance, gardening, nightly talking circles, community building, brain training, sound therapy, brain gym, gluten-free and casein-free whole-food organic meals available on site, and much more as the clients are led by their own interests and talents.

I will be leading with my own expertise, which includes being Montessori trained—as well as surviving and thriving despite emotional and financial abuse, feeling suicidal, and sustaining severe injuries from car accidents—and healing with energy and alternative medicine such as acupuncture, Chinese medicine, sound healing, and vagus nerve healing. I also have an extensive background in energy work, which is God working. I believe in God, and my take is that healing comes from God.

I believe in ancient wisdom. I appreciate land-based people's connection to Spirit. It is beautiful, it needs to be respected, and we can all learn from it. I will welcome indigenous leaders and teachers into the villages, and respectfully ask them to co-lead us into a better future to honor and renew the land.

This is no longer a lovely thought or idea, but rather it is imperative to our survival. If we don't wake up and smell the espresso, we are going to choke to death on our own garbage.

Bringing in the divine male and female as one unified entity that co-creates with God will bring healing to humans and our planet, and will bring in the new earth. We are at a crossroads where humanity has a choice. Do we choose the path of division, us versus them, male versus female, colors versus colors, beings consumed by power and greed versus the young, less empowered, and pure beings of the earth?

The answer for our survival is uniting to save and heal our planet. It is uniting as divine male and female to co-create with Spirit rather than destroying each other in the process of fighting and division.

Flashback Message

I was an outdoor-loving ten-year-old relaxing in the grass under a giant oak tree with my rabbit friend. Next to this glorious tree, a very tall birdhouse stood that housed a flock of purple martins. Birdsong filled the air. The tree lovingly held a rope swing that my dad had put up for us. I could smell the lilacs blooming and the scent from the apple trees. My beloved pony, Taffy, was close by.

I was in my element, free to be one with my Creator and the creatures so lovingly created by Him, to feel at one with all of it, all Spirit/Source/God, free to listen, to learn, and to grow. It was on this glorious midsummer day when I heard in my spirit, "The gentle people will inherit the earth."

I then saw a vision of paradise returned, and all the beautiful souls who were gentle to the earth were there. These souls were indigenous and others who were like them. There was more beauty than can be described in words. I also heard in my spirit:

"The gentle people will heal the earth. The earth will heal the gentle people. The gentle people will heal each other. And the earth will heal the gentle people. There is no end to this circle."

I felt a deep and powerful calling to protect the earth and to learn more about the gentle people. I received this message in my spirit as a child, and God let me know this was a gift and that my mission had only just begun. What I heard and saw changed my life forever.

I am here to serve the gentle people. My clients may or may not have any of these labels: autism spectrum, neurodivergent, attention-deficit disorder (ADD), pervasive developmental disorder (PDD), attention-deficit/hyperactivity disorder (ADHD), learning disability (LD), intellectual and developmental disability (IDD), dyslexia, empath, introvert, gifted, talented, out of the box, sensory dysfunction, traumatic brain injury (TBI).

My Why

I share with you, dear relatives, that I serve God and am passionately in love with His creation and His creatures. He never gave us permission to abuse them. I especially love horses (and dogs, butterflies, eagles, owls, dolphins, wolves, bears, elephants, sea turtles, otters, and so many more!).

My heart breaks as I see one of God's most beautiful angelic creatures, the horse, so horrifically abused and misunderstood, and I intend to create a sanctuary for them as well as create a treatment center for all of us to heal together.

My greatest why—my treasure, my sunshine, my greatest teacher of wisdom, grace, and miracles, and everything that is most important in life—is my daughter. Ever since her western medicine diagnosis of autism, I became obsessed with learning everything I could about it, and how to create the best possible life I could for her. I spent hours online, reading books, on the phone talking to experts, and searching everywhere I went for what I call RNAs.

RNAs are what I call Random Neighborhood Advocates, which are random people that I and I. met that "got it." They had the special sauce. It wasn't about a degree, a drug, a cure, knowledge, or some other ego-tripping thing. It was rather a simple knowing of how to *love* another human being, with a genuine, open heart, curiosity, compassion, and *zero* judgment.

This *love* is the ultimate healing medicine. This is the way, for example, a dog or horse loves a human despite our faults. We come into this world knowing how to love in this way, and some rare adults hold on to that knowledge and radiate a purity of heart out into the darkness, touching seeking hearts with gold, creating a positive impact on the world.

This is how I and I. met some of our greatest friends along the way, how we survived a chaotic home environment, and how we healed our hearts. For example, we met Marnita at a swimming pool. She introduced us to an online school, and our kids became friends. She shared her astounding business with us, Marnita's Table, which was then in its startup phase. She hosted all-inclusive dinner parties in her own home, and it has since expanded to so much more. Millionaires and CEOs sat next to homeless people, and no one knew each other's social status.

Everyone had a voice and was given equal opportunity to speak.

We became regulars at her dinner parties, and my daughter proceeded to shatter every stereotype *while in that environment*. For example, "Autistic individuals are not social, and can't handle loud noises or crowds." How was this possible?

Because there was an atmosphere of unconditional *love* and acceptance. Everyone had a voice and a turn to speak. Everyone was welcomed as an equal. This is the *key* to all of the greatest teaching, healing, transformation, friendship, expansion of the mind, and healing of the mind, body, soul, and spirit. It's so simple yet elusive. It's unfortunately very rare in individuals and even more so in groups.

We met many other RNAs this way, which opened doors to some amazing experiences, such as martial arts, kung fu, violin lessons, math lessons, homeschool gym, play groups in the park, hip-hop dance, music, art, art lessons, a special waiter who always gave her her own table when we went out to the only restaurant that "worked" for us (and because of him, the cat lady who told us about the stars), softball, soccer, jazz and dinner with other families who "got it," and experts telling me my daughter is a visual genius (yes, I noticed that).

There is so much more to notice. There is always more. I found it ironic that I would be in doctors' offices telling them about all these things they didn't know about as if I were the one getting paid.

Or when I would talk to an expert on the phone, trying to line up a treatment, and get sabotaged by someone who had no clue or concern about what I was doing and only sought to pull me down. Despite so many challenges and difficulties along the way, we rise; I rise.

Now, as a collective, we face a time of tremendous change. There are lines that divide, and there is a third option, to rise above it all. To choose love.

Next Steps

I feel as though I have been waiting my whole life for this moment. As a visionary, it is challenging to think in steps because I can see the finished product. Going through the process is where my team comes in. As I lean into mentorship and guidance from Spirit, I am open to opportunities.

"See them not as challenges, but opportunities."

— DEAN GRAZIOSI

I have purchased forty acres in northern Minnesota to start my horse rescue and HeartMath therapy center. I am creating a yard sale fundraiser for my startup at the time of this writing. I am calling in other caring parents who want a safe, healthy, affordable home for their loved one, in a loving, sustainable community. This will become our village mastermind.

God/Spirit has shown me miracles every step of the way. Every time I have stepped out in faith, I have experienced them. You may call them synchronicities, or just coincidences. I invite you to open your mind and heart to the Great Mystery, and I promise you will be delighted and your life will improve in many ways that you never saw coming.

I hope my vision has inspired you to hope, to dream, and to move forward in seeking a better life for your family.

"Never doubt that a small group of thoughtful, committed individuals can change the world. In fact, it is the only thing that ever has."

— MARGARET MEAD

Rachel J. Becquer is a writer, artist, and founder of GreenAble Village, a community for families with special needs. You can reach Rachel at greenablevillage.com

9

CASH FLOW COMES FIRST: THE LIFEBLOOD OF ENTREPRENEURIAL

BY KRIS GARLEWICZ

I t took me years of watching business owners struggle with their finances before I realized the one thing they often neglected: cash flow. I've seen entrepreneurs become fixated on taxes, expenses, raising capital, or even the latest marketing tactics, all while ignoring the most vital piece of their business's survival—cash flow. It's the oxygen of a company, the pulse that keeps everything moving.

I learned this the hard way. Early in my career, I worked with a client who was constantly focused on new strategies to increase profits. They were obsessed with boosting sales, launching products, and cutting costs. But despite these efforts, they were always scrambling for cash. Their problems didn't come from a lack of profit, but from failing to manage the money flowing in and out of their business.

That's when it hit me: Cash flow has to come first, before any other tactic. Without it, none of the other strategies matter.

Once I showed this client how to track, manage, and forecast cash flow, everything changed. They no longer operated in a reactive state. Instead of panicking over late payments or financial shortfalls, they had a clear picture of when cash was coming in, when it was going out, and how to plan accordingly. They were able to scale their business without relying on outside funding, and they finally gained control over their operations.

What is Cash Flow?

Cash flow, simply put, is the movement of money in and out of your business. It's more than just a line item on a financial statement—it's the foundation for decision-making, investments, and growth. Too many entrepreneurs make the mistake of thinking that profits are all that matter. But while profits are important, they don't tell the full story. You can have a profitable business on paper and still go bankrupt if your cash flow isn't managed properly.

By focusing on cash flow first, you ensure that your business has the liquidity it needs to meet its obligations, invest in new opportunities, and avoid unnecessary debt or dilution of ownership.

How to Implement a Cash-Flow-First Approach

1. **Monthly Cash Flow Check-ins:** Start by scheduling a dedicated time, at least once a month, to review your cash flow. This should include looking at what's coming in, what's going out, and any upcoming expenses or payments.

2. **Automate Cash Flow Tracking:** Use tools or assign a team member to monitor cash flow in real time. This gives you an instant snapshot of where your business stands financially.

3. **Forecast Your Cash Flow:** Don't just look at past performance—project future cash flow based on expected revenues, expenses, and investments. This will allow you to make better decisions about growth, hiring, and new initiatives.

4. **Reevaluate Payment Terms:** Negotiate favorable payment terms with customers and suppliers to keep cash flowing smoothly. Aim to collect cash quickly while extending your outgoing payments where possible.

5. **Cash Flow as a Decision-Making Tool:** Every tactic you use in your business—whether it's marketing, sales, product expansion, or hiring—

should be evaluated through the lens of cash flow. Ask yourself, "How will this affect my cash flow in the next month, quarter, or year?" If you don't know, pause and calculate before moving forward.

Cash Flow Versus Other Tactics

Now, don't get me wrong—tactics like marketing, tax planning, and cost management are all important. But they are secondary to cash flow. Too often, entrepreneurs chase tactics without considering the bigger picture. For instance, I've seen businesses invest heavily in marketing campaigns, only to find themselves short on cash when it's time to pay their vendors. It's like building a beautiful house but forgetting to lay a solid foundation.

Cash flow provides the freedom to experiment with these tactics. When your cash flow is under control, you can confidently invest in marketing, expand your product line, or even acquire another business without risking your financial stability. Without it, every move feels like a gamble.

Cash Flow is Freedom

The true power of cash flow is that it gives you control. It allows you to make decisions from a position of strength, not desperation. Whether you're running a high-growth tech startup or a local service business, cash flow gives you the freedom to scale at your own pace.

There's a common misconception that businesses need to constantly raise capital to grow. But when you focus on cash flow, you may find that you don't need outside funding at all. Instead of diluting ownership or giving up control, you can use your cash flow to fund growth internally. You're no longer at the mercy of investors, banks, or external forces. You're in the driver's seat.

Cash Flow in Real Time

To effectively manage cash flow, you need to make it a regular habit. In my own business, I review cash flow on the first of every month. I move columns, highlight changes, and assess where improvements can be made. But I also recommend a brief weekly check-in. Just seven minutes every Monday can give you a clear picture of your cash position and help you avoid surprises.

This practice is especially important in today's fast-moving business environment. Inflation, interest rate hikes, and fluctuating customer demand can all impact your cash flow in unexpected ways. By staying on top of it, you're always prepared to adjust and make informed decisions.

The Moral of the Story: Cash Flow Equals Freedom

In the end, mastering cash flow gives you freedom—the freedom to make strategic choices, invest in your business, and weather financial storms without panic. Cash flow isn't just a tactic; it's the most critical element of business success. It allows you to make decisions from a place of strength, not desperation. Prioritize cash flow, and everything else will fall into place.

Kris is The Financial Bodyguard to Family-Owned Businesses, author and founder of ProsperiFi. You can reach Kris at Prosperi-Fi.com/CFbook

10

YOU ARE NOT ALONE

BY VIOLET MEUTER

Growing up in a small midwestern town has its advantages and disadvantages. Born in the U.S. to European parents from Switzerland, my sisters and I were taught at an early age that it takes hard work and dedication to succeed in life.

My father was a cheese maker by trade, my mother a homemaker and full-time mom to four girls born within five years of one another. Did we drive her crazy at times? Well, yes—but that's when basements come in handy in the Chicagoland area, because in addition to tornado protection, that's where we were sent when my wonderful, and some-times stressed-out, mom needed some peace and quiet.

Dad taught us if you're going to do something, you need to do it right—always. With care, precision, and quality—otherwise, it is not worth doing.

Although my dad's father owned and operated a cheese factory in Switzerland, both parents passed away when my dad was a young man. And when my dad met my mom, it was love at first sight, and their strong sense of adventure brought them to the United States.

We were taught that the best way to make a living was to work for a good company. Because then, when you honed your craft, excelled in your work, and were dedicated to your job and company—your reward was a secure job, including benefits and pension, for life. It was the responsible, and safe, thing to do.

So, you could safely say that entrepreneurship was not heard of in my U.S.-based family. As my sisters and I grew older, deciding what we wanted to "do" in life meant honing our skills, getting an education, and going to work for Uncle Sam. And I did just that at the age of fifteen. Then, at the age of eighteen, I secured my first information technology job as a programmer analyst for enterprise business systems—and loved it. It's great to find something you're good at—and pays very well too!

But I guess you could say that I was a bit of a rebel and a very independent spirit from a young age. After many family vacations to California, and loving every minute of them, I moved out of the Swiss chalet-inspired home that my parents built in the northern Chicago suburbs, and set a course to southern California. And that is when my life changed in many ways.

Have you ever wanted to start a successful business as an entrepreneur but were afraid to do so because your family didn't "get" you? Or, have you already tried to start your own business and failed because your family saw you struggle and told you it's better and "safer" to get a "real" job? Well, if so, you're not alone.

Becoming a successful entrepreneur takes courage and dedication. And one of the things I learned, having started a successful million-dollar IT consulting company at the age of twenty-nine and operated it for more than seven years with four business partners, was that having a support network is *extremely important* for entrepreneurs both starting and growing a business.

The Importance of a Support Network

Having a strong support network can make the difference between starting the business of your dreams or sitting on the sidelines day after day, year after year, watching other entrepreneurs take the plunge and enjoy a life of freedom. And those that are successful in starting and growing a business always have a support network in place. Here's why it's so important:

• **Guidance and Mentorship:** Seeking out experienced mentors in the area of your business interests can provide you with valuable advice, helping you avoid common pitfalls and make smarter decisions.

- **Emotional Support:** Entrepreneurship can be stressful and isolating. Having people to talk to, share your challenges with, and receive encouragement from is critical to supporting your mental health and motivation.

- **Opportunities and Connections:** A strong network can help you access new opportunities, including referrals and introductions to potential clients, investors, suppliers, and/or partnerships.

- **Collaboration and Ideation:** Your network can act as a sounding board for new ideas, offering different ways of looking at opportunities and solutions you might not have considered.

- **Accountability:** Sharing your goals and progress with trusted people can hold you accountable, keeping you focused and on track—both critical components to building a successful business.

How to Build and Leverage a Support Network

So, what are the best ways for you to build and leverage a support network? Here are some methods that many of my clients and colleagues use, and that I too continue to use in my business that make a huge difference in my mindset, business strategy, execution, and growth—and keep me "in the game" even when faced with challenges.

Thanks to technology, you too can easily use these effective processes and resources while in the comfort of your own home, or while out in your local community and attending live events. You have the best of all worlds at your side!

• **Join Entrepreneurial Communities:** Online platforms like LinkedIn, Reddit, and industry-specific groups offer spaces to connect with like-minded entrepreneurs, share insights, and learn from each other. Leveraging social media platforms offers opportunities to follow and engage with industry experts, join business-related groups, and share knowledge.

• **Attend Networking Events and Conferences:** In-person events, trade shows, or virtual conferences are great ways to meet potential mentors, partners, or collaborators. These events often provide valuable learning opportunities as well.

• **Find a Mentor or Coach:** Seeking out a mentor or hiring a business coach can provide personalized guidance. A mentor who has been through the entrepreneurial journey can offer advice tailored to your specific needs and challenges.

• **Join a Mastermind Group:** Mastermind groups are small, focused groups of entrepreneurs who meet regularly to share ideas, challenges, and solutions. These groups embrace collaboration, peer support, and accountability.

• **Utilize Local Business Networks:** Most cities have local chambers of commerce, business development centers, or entrepreneurial networks that provide resources and networking opportunities for small business owners.

• **Participate in Incubators or Accelerators:** These

programs not only provide funding and resources but also a network of fellow entrepreneurs, investors, and mentors that can significantly accelerate your business growth.

• **Seek Support From Family and Friends**: While professional support is important, family and friends can provide emotional backing, helping you stay resilient when challenges arise.

• **Collaborate With Other Entrepreneurs**: Collaborating with other businesses, whether through partnerships, co-marketing, or cross-promotion, can help you build relationships and grow your network organically.

• **Volunteer or Offer Help to Others**: By offering your expertise and support to others in your network, you'll build strong relationships based on mutual respect and trust, which often leads to reciprocal opportunities.

Improving Your Support Networking Chops

Becoming a better networker is a valuable skill for entrepreneurs, as it can open doors to new opportunities, partnerships, and mentorship. Effective networking is about building genuine relationships rather than just accumulating contacts. Here are key strategies to become a better networker:

• **Focus on Building Authentic Relationships**: Networking is not about collecting business cards; it's about establishing meaningful connections. Take a genuine interest in others, listen to their stories, and look for ways to help them without expecting anything in return. Authenticity builds trust and long-lasting relationships.

• **Improve Your Listening Skills**: Great networkers listen more than they talk. Practice active listening by giving the person you're speaking with your full attention. Ask open-ended questions to better understand their needs, goals, and challenges, which can lead to deeper and more valuable conversations.

• **Be Proactive in Offering Value**: Think about how you can help others in your network, whether it's by sharing useful resources, offering advice, or making introductions. Networking is a two-way street, and offering value will make others more willing to support you in return.

• **Follow Up and Stay in Touch**: After meeting someone, follow up with a personalized message or email to keep the conversation going. Mention something specific from your conversation to show that you were paying attention. Periodically check in with your contacts to nurture the relationship, even if there's no immediate need for their help.

• **Prepare a Clear Elevator Pitch**: Have a concise, compelling introduction ready for when people ask about you or your business. Focus on what you do, who you serve, and the value you offer. This helps others understand what you're about and makes you more memorable.

• **Diversify Your Network**: Don't limit yourself to just people in your target industry. Expand your network to include professionals from different sectors, industries, and backgrounds. A diverse network provides new perspectives and opens doors to unique opportunities you may not have considered.

• **Be Patient and Persistent**: Building a strong network takes time. Be patient, and don't rush the process. Stay consistent with your networking efforts, and don't get discouraged if you don't see immediate results. Relationships take time to develop, but they can provide lasting value over time.

• **Practice Good Networking Etiquette**: Being polite, respectful, and professional in all interactions is essential. Avoid being too transactional or pushy when asking for help. Always be mindful of other people's time, and express gratitude when someone helps you.

• **Be Consistent and Stay Visible**: Consistency is key in networking. Attend events, stay active on social media, and engage with your contacts regularly. Staying visible helps keep you top of mind when opportunities arise or when others need someone with your skills or expertise.

By following these strategies and staying genuine in your approach, you can become a more effective networker, build valuable connections, and create a strong, supportive network that benefits both your personal and business growth.

Conclusion

Building a strong support network can make the difference between starting or not starting your dream business, and significantly and positively impacting your success as an entrepreneur and business owner. I have made a point to leverage each of the above support activities, and can truly say without the support of my network, including my business coaches and fellow entrepreneur colleagues, I would not be where I am today.

Just as my team and I coach, advise, and assist clients in billion-dollar organizations and growing SMBs to assess opportunities to implement artificial intelligence (AI) and procedures to gain productivity, efficiency, reduce errors and costs, increase customer satisfaction and retention, develop business strategy, and substantially grow their net profits, so are my own coaches and entrepreneurial colleagues key to supporting my personal and business growth through collaboration, sharing ideas, strategies, connections, and referrals.

Not only has leveraging a support network been critical to my belief that I could be the first in my direct family to start and operate a thriving business that I loved, this support continues to help me maintain emotional resilience and navigate the ever-changing challenges of entrepreneurship. And now, so can you!

Take the next steps, and get out there today to begin experiencing the benefits, pride, service, mission, and support of sustainable and profitable entrepreneurship! And while you're at it, build a solid success network for life.

Violet is a passionate and accomplished entrepreneur, IT executive, author, award-winning tech copywriter, business strategist, certified AI business coach and consultant. You can reach Violet at QuantumMindset.com

11

SEEK FIRST TO UNDERSTAND, THEN TO BE UNDERSTOOD

BY MATT COOPER

Stephen Covey's Timeless Principle

Writing this chapter brings me back to an early childhood challenge that echoes the principles we're exploring. At the tender age of four or five, I faced a daily ordeal that seemed impossible. Every morning, my refusal to go to kindergarten was not just a whim but a silent and sometimes not-so-silent scream against an oppressor. This resistance wasn't mere child's play; it was a battle of wills, with my adamant refusal becoming a recurring theme, infuriating those closest to me. This cycle of resistance and insistence wove a fabric of tension that neither side could unravel.

The turning point was as gentle as it was profound. My mother, with her innate empathy, kneeled to my level and asked, "Why don't you want to go to school, Matthew?" That simple question pierced the veil of my fears, revealing the truth: my terror of the classroom closet where my teacher would confine me as a punitive measure. This confession, a stark revelation of a child's inner turmoil, led to significant changes—among them, a swift switch in schools.

This episode from my youth poignantly embodies Covey's principle of "seek first to understand, then to be understood." My mother's method, marked by empathetic listening and genuine concern, didn't just unearth the reasons behind my behavior; it fostered a solution that altered the trajectory of my education. However, the fear she uncovered that day was so deeply rooted that it lingers with me even now, manifesting as extreme claustrophobia. It's a powerful testament to the impact of truly understanding another's perspective—not only in resolving immediate issues but in addressing the lasting effects of our deepest fears.

Practical Tips for Empathetic Listening

Empathetic listening is a skill that can be practiced and honed. Here are a few practical tips to help you integrate this approach into your daily interactions:

Active Listening: Commit to fully listening to the other person before formulating your response. This means avoiding interruptions and focusing entirely on what they're saying.

Ask Open-Ended Questions: Encourage deeper conversation by asking questions that require more than a yes or no answer. This helps the other person to express their thoughts and feelings more fully.

Reflect and Clarify: Summarize or paraphrase what the other person has said to ensure you've understood them correctly. This also shows that you're genuinely engaged in the conversation.

Business and Sales Applications

In the high-stakes arena of business negotiations, the principle of "seek first to understand" becomes not just a guideline but a strategy for success. Consider the case of Jordan, a procurement manager tasked with securing a vital contract for her company. The negotiations had reached a stalemate, with both sides anchored in their positions. Instead of pushing her agenda further, Jordan decided to shift the dynamics. She invited the suppliers for a casual dinner, aiming to understand their concerns and limitations beyond the negotiation table.

As they shared stories, Jordan discovered that the suppliers were worried about the feasibility of the delivery timelines, given their current capacity constraints. This was a concern Jordan's team hadn't fully appreciated. Armed with this understanding, she proposed a revised timeline that was slightly more flexible, coupled with a commitment from her company to assist in scaling the suppliers' operations. This move not only broke the deadlock but also transformed a transactional negotiation into a long-term partnership.

Jordan's willingness to listen and understand the suppliers' perspective deeply was the key to unlocking this win-win scenario, illustrating the profound impact of empathy in negotiations.

The Importance of Empathetic Listening in Sales

Empathetic listening is also the first lesson salespeople learn. It's essential to take the time to understand the customer's problem before attempting to sell a product. When a customer visits your location, it's because they have a problem they need to solve. By asking questions to uncover the customer's problem, you can present a suitable solution. Demonstrating how your product or service can resolve the customer's problem makes them much more likely to make a purchase.

In today's world, customers frequently turn to search engines for information. Marketers must grasp their target audience's challenges and use this understanding to develop a sales funnel that directs the customer through the stages of purchase while showcasing the advantages of the product or service. This automated process, when combined with the concept of scalability, embodies the core of successful digital marketing.

Miscommunication: What Can Go Wrong?

When we fail to seek understanding first, the consequences can be significant. Consider a historical example from the business world: the launch of "New Coke" in 1985. Coca-Cola introduced a new formula without fully understanding their customers' deep emotional attachment to the original product. The backlash was swift and severe, forcing the company to reintroduce "Coca-Cola Classic" just a few months later. This costly misstep illustrates how a lack of empathetic listening can cause misunderstandings and damage relationships, even for a brand as powerful as Coca-Cola.

Empathy in Leadership

Empathetic listening isn't just for sales or negotiations; it's a critical component of effective leadership. Great leaders use empathy to connect with their teams, inspire action, and foster a positive work environment. For instance, Howard Schultz, the former CEO of Starbucks, is known for his empathetic leadership style. He prioritized understanding the needs and concerns of his employees, which helped build a strong, loyal workforce and contributed to the company's success. Empathy in leadership not only boosts morale but also drives better decision-making and innovation.

The Neuroscience of Listening

The practice of empathetic listening isn't just good communication; it's rooted in the way our brains are wired. Neuroscience research has shown that when we listen empathetically, mirror neurons in our brains activate, allowing us to feel what others are feeling. This neural mirroring helps us connect on a deeper emotional level, fostering mutual understanding and trust. Understanding the science behind empathy can motivate us to develop this skill further, knowing that it has a profound impact on our relationships and interactions.

Transitioning to Nonverbal Communication

As we shift from the profound impact of empathetic listening in personal and professional scenarios, it's essential to recognize that communication is more than just words. The unspoken elements—body language, tone of voice, and facial expressions—are powerful tools that can either enhance or undermine our message. Just as understanding others lays the foundation for effective dialogue, mastering these nonverbal cues sharpens our ability to convey meaning, ensuring that our intentions are not lost in translation.

The Power of Body Language

Body language is a powerful communicator, revealing our true feelings and intentions. An open stance, with arms uncrossed and palms visible, signals openness and receptivity, inviting others into a space of trust and collaboration. Conversely, crossed arms suggest defensiveness or resistance, even if your words convey a different message. To foster an environment of understanding, practice adopting a posture that reflects your intent to engage and connect.

The Tone of Voice: The Invisible Hand of Persuasion

Our tone of voice can soothe, motivate, challenge, or undermine our spoken words. It's not just what we say but how we say it that shapes the listener's perception. A calm, steady tone suggests confidence and reliability, while fluctuations can emphasize key points, making your message more memorable. By being mindful of your tone, you can enhance the clarity and impact of your communication.

Facial Expressions: Windows to the Soul

Facial expressions are immediate indicators of our emotions and reactions. A genuine smile, for instance, can build rapport and ease tension, signaling friendliness and openness. However, mismatched expressions—such as a frown while agreeing—can confuse and alienate your audience.

Cultivating awareness of your facial expressions ensures that they complement rather than contradict your words.

Aligning Nonverbal Cues With Your Communication Goals

Consistency between verbal and nonverbal messages is key to harnessing the full potential of nonverbal communication. This alignment reinforces your message, building credibility and trust. Practice in front of a mirror or record yourself to become more aware of your nonverbal cues and adjust them to better support your communication objectives.

"Sharpen the Saw": Embracing Continuous Evolution in Communication

This colorful Covey metaphor is not merely advice but a philosophy for sustained self-improvement. It encompasses the holistic enhancement of our physical, social, emotional, mental, and spiritual well-being. This metaphor serves as a critical foundation for advancing our communication skills, inviting us into an ongoing journey of self-reflection and growth.

As we traverse this path, we encounter two significant landmarks: the "Woodshed" and the "Theatre of the Mind." The Woodshed symbolizes a place of diligent practice and perseverance, where efforts are honed and skills are refined through repetition. Analogous to a musician tirelessly practicing scales or an athlete undergoing rigorous training, the Woodshed represents our commitment to the meticulous improvement of our communicative abilities.

Simultaneously, the Theatre of the Mind introduces us to the realm of mental rehearsal, a space where imagination and reality blur. Here, we engage in the deliberate practice of visualizing successful communication scenarios, from persuasive speeches to empathetic conversations. This practice is grounded in the neuroscience of skill acquisition, specifically the concept of myelin formation, as explored in Daniel Coyle's *The Talent Code*. Myelin, a fatty substance that envelops neural pathways, strengthens and speeds up electrical impulses between neurons, thereby enhancing our ability to perform complex tasks with greater efficiency and precision.

Empathy in Digital Communication

In today's digital age, much of our communication happens through text, emails, or social media. Applying empathetic listening and understanding in digital communication can be challenging but is no less important. Mindful word choice and tone in emails or messages can convey empathy, and taking the time to consider the other person's perspective before responding can prevent miscommunication. Digital communication might lack the richness of face-to-face interactions, but with careful attention to these details, it can still foster strong, empathetic connections.

Reflection and Application

The intersection of the Woodshed and the Theatre of the Mind results in a profound impact of both physical and mental practice on our communicative prowess. By cross-referencing Coyle's insights, we gain a deeper understanding of how diligent practice, both in action and in thought, can fortify the neural pathways that underpin our ability to communicate effectively.

Reflecting on my journey, from overcoming early educational challenges to navigating the highs and lows of a professional career, I recognize the power of continuous learning and the humility it instills. Each step forward, marked by moments of uncertainty and discovery, has been a testament to the transformative power of striving to understand before being understood.

Conclusion: Key Takeaways

1. **Empathy as a Foundation:** Understanding others is not just a principle but a practice that can transform personal relationships and business outcomes.

2. **Nonverbal Communication:** Mastering body language, tone of voice, and facial expressions can significantly enhance the effectiveness of your communication.

3. **Continuous Improvement:** Embrace the philosophy of "sharpen the saw" by consistently refining your communica-

tion skills through both physical practice and mental rehearsal.

4. Practical Application: Whether in personal interactions or professional negotiations, the ability to listen, understand, and align your verbal and nonverbal cues will set you apart as a communicator.

5. Empathy in Digital Communication: Apply empathetic listening even in digital communications by being mindful of word choice, tone, and the other person's perspective.

Interactive Element: Reflection Exercise

Before closing the chapter, take a moment to reflect on a recent conversation where you might have listened more empathetically. How could the outcome have changed if you had practiced active listening, asked open-ended questions, or reflected and clarified what the other person was saying? Challenge yourself to apply these principles in your next interaction and observe the impact.

This journey of understanding and communication is ongoing. As you continue to practice these principles, you will find that each step forward not only improves your interactions but also enriches your overall life experience.

Matt Cooper is an entrepreneur, best-selling author, and radio personality. You can reach Matt at Matt@MattCooper.ca

12

ENTREPRENEURS ARE DREAM BUILDERS

BY DANE A. DEUTSCH

In the earliest days I can remember, my parents were dream builders. My mother and father didn't just talk about dreams—they lived them every single day. They believed in the power of dreaming big and instilled that belief in me. From the time I was a little kid, I dreamed of being like my mom and dad. They'd always tell me, "You can accomplish anything you put your mind to." Looking back, I think they were talking about more than just career goals. They were talking about having a great vision for life and the perseverance to see it through, no matter what.

But it wasn't just about success; it was about achieving success with honor. My parents made sure I understood that. They instilled in me the importance of integrity, teaching me that achieving my goals without honor wasn't success at all. To demonstrate this, let me tell you a story about my mom that left a profound impact on me and remains as vivid today as when she first shared it with me.

My mom is a person of honor, someone who leads by example. She doesn't just talk the talk; she walks the walk. When I was in the seventh grade, my mom gave me a book titled *Psycho-Cybernetics* by Dr. Maxwell Maltz. At first, I was puzzled. I mean, it's a book about psychology, way over the head of a typical seventh-grader. But my mom had a good reason for giving it to me. She said, "If you want to do something great in life, like be a business owner or an entrepreneur, you need to read this book. It'll help you accomplish anything you want to do."

By then, I had already watched my mom build her business from scratch—literally from scratch and from the ground up. She was a true entrepreneur! I witnessed her buying the first little arts and crafts, beads and paint, gradually expanding into what eventually became a picture-framing store. That store, The Elf Shelf, started in Brainerd, Minnesota, and thrived against all the odds. What struck me most was my mom's unshakeable belief that she could do anything she put her mind to. If she dreamed of something, that dream became a reality.

She often told me the story of how she started The Elf Shelf with just $1,000 from my dad. At first, he wasn't sure she could make it work, but he gave her the money and said, "When that $1,000 is gone, that's all you're going to get." So, she had to make it work. She had to make a living and

The Entrepreneur's Playbook

generate revenue before that $1,000 ran out—and that's exactly what she did.

Against all odds, in the early seventies, my mom launched her little arts and crafts store. Many people doubted she could succeed, but she did more than that—she thrived. After my dad retired from the US Air Force, he joined my mom in the business and started the professional picture frame part of the business. The Elf Shelf became a well-known store in Brainerd, Minnesota, respected by the community. My mom's entrepreneurship wasn't just about making money; it was about showing what dedication, belief, and honor could achieve.

Years later, my parents moved back to their hometown in Rice Lake, Wisconsin, where they opened another picture-framing shop. They extended their arts and crafts business into this new venture as well and called it Deutsch's Picture Framing. Today, it's known as Nature's Gallery, but the legacy of what my mom and dad built is still there, serving people across the United States with professional arts and crafts as well as picture-framing services.

My mom didn't just impact the people of Brainerd; she left her mark on the community in Rice Lake as well. She made my dad a believer in the power of dreams. As Walt Disney famously said, "If you can dream it, you can do it."[1] My mom lived by that philosophy, and she taught me to do

1. "A Quote by Walt Disney Company." *Goodreads*, Goodreads, www.-goodreads.com/quotes/24673-if-you-can-dream-it-you-can-do-it-always.

the same. Dreams aren't just fantasies or wishes. They're blueprints for what we can achieve if we have the courage and determination to pursue them.

That's what being a dream builder is all about. It's not just about having dreams but making them come true. It's about believing in yourself and working tirelessly until you achieve what you set out to do. Most importantly, it's about doing it with integrity and honor so that when you look back, you know you've achieved something truly great.

My mother's lesson about building a business as an entrepreneur with grit and resilience was a key reason my wife and I decided to start our own business after leaving the Air Force. We came back to our roots in Wisconsin to open a gymnastics training center. Inspired by my parents, we wanted to be dream builders too—not just for ourselves but for the young gymnasts who would walk through our doors.

Before opening our gym on June 1, 1990, we knew our mission was more than just training young athletes. It was about weaving a thread of character, leadership, and moral values into their lives—all without explicitly saying so. In our gym, banners proudly display virtues like trustworthiness, respect, responsibility, fairness, caring, and citizenship, quietly whispering the deeper purpose we are passionately pursuing.

Starting our gym in a small town of fewer than 9,000 residents, where my parents had lived and grown up, was both exciting and nerve-racking. Shortly after opening, I was invited to speak at a local men's club meeting. It was a great opportunity to share our dream, our vision, and our new business venture. But before I even got a chance to start speaking, one of the town's leaders made a comment that briefly shook my confidence. He said, "You won't last six months."

Imagine hearing that when you're bubbling with excitement and purpose. But if there's one thing we didn't lack, it was grit. We were determined to prove him wrong. My wife and I didn't just survive those first six months—we've thrived in our little gym business for over three decades. We've impacted and touched the lives of thousands of children and families, imparting not only gymnastics skills but also lessons in leadership, communication, and, most importantly, character.

The statistics can be daunting: "According to the U.S. Bureau of Labor Statistics (BLS), approximately 20% of new businesses fail during the first two years of being open, 45% during the first five years, and 65% during the first 10 years. Only 25% of new businesses make it to 15 years or more."[2]

It takes more than technical skills to survive in any business over the long haul. People skills like teamwork, communication, and leadership are crucial. But what truly makes the difference are character skills like grit, courage, and integrity.

---

2. Deane, Michael T. "Top 6 Reasons New Businesses Fail." *Investopedia*, Investopedia, www.investopedia.com/financial-edge/1010/top-6-reasons-new-businesses-fail.aspx.

Negative feedback comes in many forms, but staying positive and looking for the good in every situation is vital. My mom taught me this lesson time and again. Negative feedback can be constructive if we interpret and use it correctly. Her resilience taught me that the cards might be stacked against us, but with determination, we can overcome any obstacle.

That's what we did with our gymnastics center. Despite the early doubt, we leaned into our commitment and passion. Our dedication not only allowed us to stay afloat but to become a cornerstone in our community. We learned to interpret challenges as opportunities for growth with the same perseverance my mother showed when building and championing her business.

What's remarkable about dream builders like my mom and dad is the ripple effect they create in making a difference for others through their entrepreneurship and dreams. My mom's passion and determination inspired everyone around her, including my dad, and that's the legacy we strive to build in our community. We want to be the hope and inspiration for others and make a difference for them by showing them that dreams are achievable with the right mix of hard work, honor, and integrity.

As I grew up, I carried my mom's lessons with me. I pursued my dreams with the same tenacity and honor she showed me. Her example taught me that setbacks are just stepping stones to success and that the only limits are the ones we place on ourselves.

Today, as I reflect on my journey, I realize that my parents were more than dream builders. They were "architects of possibility," crafting a world where dreams became the reality. Their legacy isn't just in the businesses they built or the communities they served; it's in the lives they touched and the inspiration they passed on to others and even to me as I learned to dream big and chase those dreams with all my heart.

Being a dream builder is about more than dreaming; it's about building a life of purpose and impact. It's about believing in yourself and working tirelessly to turn your visions into reality. My parents showed me that true success is measured not just by what you achieve but by how you achieve it.

Today, we have built and owned six businesses, each of which was built from scratch as true entrepreneurs: from our dreams to our passionate vision to practical reality.

Their journey taught me that with honor, integrity, and relentless pursuit, anything is possible. And that's the legacy I hope to pass on to others—a legacy of dreaming big, working hard, and building a future filled with endless possibilities.

Here's to you—the dreamer, the visionary, the one who dares to take risks and turn possibilities into reality. You have the power to become a dream builder, chart your course, and create a future that not only fulfills your dreams and goals but also paints your passion and inspires others to do the same. Remember to tackle your life and entrepreneurial challenges head-on, learn from any setbacks that might happen, and be passionate about moving yourself forward. Never give up! Remember, each of our personal journeys starts with the courage to dream big and take the first step.

Now is your time to make your mark, transform your dreams into reality, and leave a lasting legacy of impact and innovation. Take the leap, trust in your vision, and become the entrepreneur you are destined to be.

The world is waiting for you to make a difference with your brilliance—go out there and shine!

Come journey with Dane, a visionary entrepreneur and 35-year business owner of five companies, with unparalleled experience and expertise. Connect with Dane at https://coach.lmdc.us/DaneDigBizCard

13

GET YOUR M.B.A. (MUST BRING ATTENTION)

BY GEORGE LUI

If you were to gather a roomful of successful entrepreneurs and ask them to list what they believe to be the most critical business and marketing skills, what attributes would you expect to be on that list?

Being social media savvy? Or having excellent sales skills? How about being a master networker?

Yes, they're essential business skills. However, one skill should be at the top of your list.

It's the ability to build a mailing list—a superpower that entrepreneurs can't afford to ignore.

Do you want to generate more leads, grow your sales, and increase your profits? Of course, you do—who wouldn't? The most predictable way to do this is to build a mailing list of prospects and customers.

You may have heard the saying, "The money is on the

list." Building a mailing list also opens up the opportunity of joint ventures with other entrepreneurs and can help you sell your business for a healthy profit in the future.

Having a great mailing list is like having a private cash machine for your business. When you need to increase your profits, you can mail your list with an irresistible offer and watch the sales roll in.

I once saw Daniel Priestley on the YouTube channel "Diary of a C.E.O." describing how Elon Musk validated the idea of the Tesla Model 3 and the Cybertruck just by using a waiting list, which is another term for a mailing list. If it worked for Elon, it could also work for you.

A mailing list aims to facilitate direct marketing, maintain customer relationships, and drive sales through targeted email campaigns.

The potential losses from not having a mailing list can be catastrophic. You may have a fantastic product or service, but without a mailing list, you must rely on expensive advertising to get sales.

Also, imagine having a following on social media platforms such as YouTube and Facebook. Then, one day, you get banned from posting content—or worse, your account gets deleted. How would your customers be able to receive updates from you if they're not on your mailing list?

Regardless of the type of business, whether it's the local cafe, a social media agency, or a socks supplier, having a mailing list makes good business sense. It is an asset that's worth growing.

Now that we've established how valuable a mailing list is, the next step is to discover how to build and grow one.

Today, I want to discuss three popular methods that have proven to deliver an M.B.A. (Must Bring Attention) for businesses.

M.B.A. Tip #1 - Conduct A Prize-Winning Competition

When I ran a mortgage brokering business, my mailing list grew whenever I held a competition offering the lucky winner an overseas trip plus additional spending money. The success came from incentivizing the entrant whenever they gave a referral in exchange for an extra entry into the competition. This had a snowball effect when the original referral also offered another set of referrals I could contact.

The strategy of running a competition to build a mailing list has existed for decades, and that's because it just works. It's fun to participate, and if done correctly, not only can it grow your mailing list, but it has the potential to create a buzz around your brand.

A well-executed competition must have these elements:

The Prize

Choose a prize that would make sense to your target audience and, most importantly, relate to your business. If you are a gym owner, offer the winner a three-month personal trainer membership.

However, giving away a three-month supply of donuts may give a different message.

What kind of prizes would work for your business? Go and brainstorm and make a list of potential prizes.

Low Barrier Of Entry

The message here is simple: Do not make your potential prospects jump too many hurdles to enter the competition, as this can quickly kill their interest.

A name, email address, and even a contact number will suffice; try to ask for only a little information—make it quick and easy.

People crave convenience, so consider using a QR code to redirect visitors to your competition page instead of forcing them to type in the website address.

Due Diligence

This is especially true if the prize is cash related and you want to respect local laws.

The terms and conditions of the competition should be very clear. They should define the duration of the competition, the rules of entry, and how the winner will be chosen. Consider outsourcing to companies specializing in running competitions, especially if you don't have the luxury of learning the craft from scratch.

Promotional plan

Let's start with the low-hanging fruit: Let your mailing list know you are running a competition and encourage them to tell their family and friends about it. This is the power of having a loyal base. Social media platforms are famous for promoting competitions, so take advantage of the technology.

Even if you are not IT savvy, leverage freelancers on sites like Fiverr or Upwork to do the legwork. Remember, no matter how fantastic the competition prize is, if nobody knows about it, then you are looking at a white elephant, so treat your marketing activities with tremendous respect.

M.B.A. Tip #2 - Press Releases

Press releases have been around for a long time. They're simple to implement and can work for just about any business. They can open the door to featuring your company on local TV and in newspapers, trade journals, and magazines.

A press release is generally centered around the following:

1. New product/service launch (a new self-published service).
2. Company news (mergers, acquisitions, partnerships).
3. Event announcements (a new airline operation).

4. 4. Awards or achievements (coverage of the small business award).
5. New hire announcements (movers and shakers).
6. Financial reports (franchise is expanding nationwide).

Getting a press release written for your business is simple. On one occasion, I teamed up with another entrepreneur and hired a PR agency. The agency interviewed us and then wrote the press release. Once we approved it, it was distributed to various media outlets in our city.

This resulted in a local nightly news channel running a story about our services, and afterward, leads flowed into our businesses. Now, that's what I call an M.B.A.

Journalists are constantly hungry for content, so as business owners, this presents a tremendous opportunity to grow our company profile. One platform facilitating such connections is H.A.R.O. (Help A Reporter Out), which now operates under the name Connectively and is owned by Cision.

Alternatively, PRLog also offers a free press release distribution service that you can test-drive. Even if these platforms are unsuitable for your liking, it's relatively easy to track down the contact details of your local newspaper journalist or a blog article writer to introduce yourself. The key is to reach out and make yourself known consistently.

While on the subject of a well-crafted press release, here are some ideas for you to consider before you send off that email:

1 Aim to coincide with something newsworthy. Artificial Intelligence is hot right now, so do you have a product/service that fits the trend?

2 A press release must always be written in the third person, whether singular or plural—"it" or "they," as appropriate.

3 Do you have exclusive content to give journalists, something unique they can't get elsewhere?

4 It's commonplace for businesses to include a press release kit (a media kit) on their website for journalists to download.

The kit usually contains most of the following items:

1. A press release: A well-written, concise announcement of your news because journalists are time-poor.
2. Company background: A quick summary of your business.
3. Founder/executive bios: Profiles of key team members only.
4. Fact sheet: Back up your claims with solid numbers.
5. High-resolution media assets: Logos, product photos, team photos.
6. Video clips: Product/service demos or company overview videos.
7. Glowing customer reviews or case studies.
8. FAQ section: Aim to list ten questions.

9. Your best contact information.

10. Ensure your media kit is mobile-friendly.

The benefits of using a press release are enormous. It increases your brand's visibility to journalists and potential prospects when done correctly. It can also raise your credibility as a subject matter expert, and it's another excellent way to grow your mailing list.

M.B.A. Tip #3 - Authoring A Book

In this noisy world of social media postings, a book (preferably in physical form) can generate attraction. Imagine you're on a flight, and the person next to you passes you a typical business card. That's a nice gesture, so you thank the person and slip the card into your pocket, and that's the end of that.

However, what would be your reaction if you were handed a copy of a book the person wrote? I suspect you would be shocked and curious about this person. That's an M.B.A. right there because they've got your attention. I guarantee that the book will have a longer shelf life and is less likely to be thrown away than a plain business card.

Take a look at just some of the benefits of what a book can do for your brand:

Cementing Your Authority

A book persuades people's perception to accept you as

someone who has extensive knowledge from experiences in your field. People are hungry for information and answers. Your book is the solution provider, and you, as the author, can become a people magnet.

Speaking Engagements

When your book truly takes off, be prepared to be invited to be a guest speaker. What better way to wow your audience than to share some of the valuable contents of the book and give copies away?

Even if you are not paid to speak, the publicity generated will be worthwhile, and you can always ask the organizer for an opportunity to sell your books at the back of the stage if you want to recuperate some of your costs.

Differentiation From Competitors

Competition is good because it means there is profit and opportunities. But it's critical not to become a "Me Too" among other players in your niche. Having a book will set you apart and give you that edge. I've encountered hundreds of self-employed mortgage brokers, but I've only known five who have authored a book, making them stand out.

Content Marketing

Specifically, I'm talking about repurposing the content.

Consider each chapter as inspiration for multiple blog posts, YouTube videos, Pinterest pins, and X tweets. Be creative and discover ways to create six months' worth of blog articles based on the book.

Interestingly, James Altucher reverse engineered the process of creating the book. In his podcast with Charlie Hoehn, James explained that his book *Choose Yourself* was based on rewriting his most successful articles into chapters for the book.

There are many schools of thought about what makes a good business book, but allow me to share my thoughts on that question.

A good book should contain the following:

1. A great title (without one, your chance of getting noticed diminishes).
2. A great book cover (ugly ones should be banned).
3. A focus on a specific problem or need of your target audience.
4. Genuine value and actionable insights provided in an engaging manner.
5. Content that is professionally edited and designed.
6. A call to action to the reader (join your mailing list).
7. Case studies of your own or real-world examples.

So there you have it—three simple yet highly powerful

M.B.A.s that you can quickly implement into your business starting this week. Remember this wise entrepreneurial maxim: "Money loves speed!"

So, which M.B.A. will you work on today?

George is an author, educator and entrepreneur based in Australia. You can reach him at www.GeorgeLui.com

14

TAKING THE PLUNGE

BY PAUL G. BRODIE

"A journey of a thousand miles begins with a single step."

— LAO TZU

The quote I just shared is over 2,000 years old and is one that I share often with my audience and clients. One of the hardest things to do when starting the journey as an entrepreneur is to take those first steps.

In June 2017, I took those first steps when I retired from teaching at forty-two years old after a nine-year career to focus on my publishing business full-time. The first year was a struggle, and I almost went out of business.

Initially, I started the business as a coaching model, as I was convinced that I could teach people how to publish and market their own book. The content I created was great, but I kept hearing the same message. I was told by many business owners that my content was great, but they did not have the time to learn how to do it.

What they suggested was that I create a done-for-you service for both book publishing and book launch marketing. What happened next changed my life. I listened to the advice they gave me and implemented it. In fall 2018, while in Las Vegas, I decided to stop my coaching program and went all in with two done-for-you services.

Within the next month, we generated significant revenue with the done-for-you book publishing and book launch marketing services. In 2019, we had our first six-figure year, and we have hit revenue records every year since. The best part was that we were able to get our clients the results they deserved, and as of writing this chapter, we have launched over 170 consecutive best-selling book launches for clients across the world in over twenty countries.

I was able to take the coaching systems that I initially implemented and tweak them for our done-for-you clients. We also were able to guarantee that all our clients would become best-selling authors as long as they had a great-looking book cover, a well-edited manuscript, and a professional-looking formatted manuscript.

The reason I wanted to share this is because taking risks is scary. I literally gambled my life savings and almost failed. The best thing I did was to take the plunge, but more importantly, I listened to my clients and prospects and implemented what they suggested. When you keep receiving the same message over and over, then you may want to lean in and implement that advice.

By using those tools, you can have the same potential for success, but the first thing you must do is to take the plunge.

Sincerely,
Paul Brodie
CEO, Brodie Consulting Group

You can get more information about how we serve our clients and also grab a free copy of my *Get Published* book at www.BrodieConsultingGroup.com.

Paul Brodie is a 21-time best selling author and CEO of Brodie Consulting. He helps people share their stories to position them as experts in their field. You can connect with Paul at www.Brodie-ConsultingGroup.com.

THE CO-AUTHOR PROJECT

Compiled By

co-author.me

Made in United States
Troutdale, OR
08/13/2025

33619315R00070